W9-DAN-434

SOME FAR COUNTRY

PARTRIDGE BOSWELL

GROLIER POETRY PRESS
Discovery Series

Acknowledgments

Thanks to the editors of periodicals in which these poems first appeared:
The American Poetry Review: Wonder; *New Delta Review*: Mangrove; *Main Street Rag*: Distances, Just Remember I Knew You When, In Hindsight, a Happy Accident; *The Larcom Review*: Iceman; *Rattle*: And Pigs May Fly; *Ekphrasis*: Midsummer Dance; *Across Borders*: The Patience of Roméo Dallaire, The Mission, The Weather in Karbala; *The Salon* and *Poetry Alive*: Reading; *Anthology of New England Writers*: After Two Lines Simultaneously Nearing the End of Books by Jean Valentine and Jane Austen; *Aethlon: The Journal of Sports Literature*: Dinner with Uncle Tom; *The MacGuffin*: Distances, Blues for M'Baïki, General Admission; *Kaleidoscope*: The Deep End; *West Wind Review*: Guard Duty; *the minnesota review*: Found; *The Hurricane Review*: The Documentarists; *Whitefish Review*: How This Next Song Came To Be; *The Literary Review* and *Backwards City Review*: Never the Twain; *Birchsong: Poetry Centered in Vermont*: Just Remember I Knew You When, Forty Words; *Salamander*: Quiz, Saltimbanques. *Slice*: Some Far Country, Six Caveats upon Entering the Kingdom of Superlatives. Certain poems were first published in the chapbook *In Hindsight, a Happy Accident* produced by Pudding House Publications, Columbus, Ohio. Lasting gratitude to Ifeanyi Menkiti and the Grolier Family for their warm embrace and steadfast support.

Grolier Poetry Press, Cambridge, Massachusetts

Cover art: Obstbäume, Gustav Klimt, private collection

Producer: Tiger Bridge Graphics

Cover design: Heron Graphic Arts

Interior design: Circumstantial Productions

ISBN: 978–0–98–893521–1

CONTENTS

INTRODUCTION

Partridge Boswell is a poet of many parts. Although his eyes are firmly focused on the foibles of America's domestic situation he has not lost sight of the world beyond America's shores. His gaze is turned here, but also there. Whether it be the spectacle of the child soldiers in Sierra Leone ("The Documentarists") or the obscenity of those floating bodies blanketing the swollen rivers of Rwanda ("The Patience of Romeo Dallaire"), Boswell bears witness to the understanding that the world is ultimately one, and that looking beyond one's backyard does not mean that one has failed to care for one's backyard. Indeed, a demand for a capacious spirit, one generous onto the entire world must be embraced as an important task for poetry today. Otherwise the local roots of the poem will ultimately fail to find an adequate basis for their own articulation. In crucial ways, it is the global that secures the local, not the other way round. My cry is a cry worthy of others' attention, not because it is my cry, but because they themselves already know what it is to cry.

I must of course confess that I am partial to this way of looking at the world, including the world of poetry. But I must continue to do so until others show me a better way of doing it. And this brings me back to Boswell and the choice of his manuscript, *Some Far Country*, for the Discovery Award. His poems claim the honor for themselves in terms of reach and in terms of lyric grace. One is able to enjoy the substance of what he has written because the poems have significance and because the writing is good, very good. Because Boswell has been able to pay homage to those facts on the ground in foreign places, I find myself taking more seriously what the poet has to say (or not say) regarding the home-grown situations. As I read "The Documentarists," "The Weather in Karbala," "The Patience of Romeo Dallaire," "Blues for M'Baiki," I find that these poems, with their echo of the tragedies of alien lands, also help me to read with more substantive human interest the domestic explorations which Boswell pursues in poems such as "Still," "Game Night at Fenway," "Dinner With Uncle Tom," "Our Little Japes."

Obviously much of what I say here is a matter of sensibility. But there is, too, the matter of craft, an area in which Boswell stands out as well. When one reads the lines of the poem "Still" and follows these up with the lines from the poem "Six Caveats Upon Entering the Kingdom of Superlatives," one gets a fuller sense of Boswell's excellence in the matter of lyric measure. I quote "Six Caveats:"

insofar the doorlight behind you
has closed its aperture

downsodeep the steep ravine
brings a bottomless sleep

oversoyonder hills eyes fold
more cloth than can be quilted

abovesohigh a throne no deity
could possibly survive the fall

moonsobright fields glow like seas
of love between continents of trees

insomuch less is more please
leave your dreams at the door

That the patterns of song are so cleverly and so appropriately married to the variety of subject matter is also evident in other places. Thus the long run-on breathless lines of "Our Little Japes" [which opens with an unforgettable quote from Quentin Crisp: "The trouble with children is that you can't return them" (p.41)] seems entirely appropriate, even perhaps unavoidable, given what the poet is about. As this poem moves to capture a certain kind of domestic misalignment primarily associated with discordant malehood, one gets the feeling that it is as if to be a man today, or a young boy growing up, is to be misaligned whenever and wherever the issue at hand is one of basic sense, maybe basic grace. Where does the responsibility lie? Where pin it? Parents often fail their children, and children fail their parents, too. And, of course, luck is part of the process, but who has any control over luck?

In reading Boswell, then, one notices how well the long poems feed seamlessly off the short, and how well the short lines of the shorter poems condense and crystalize what the long poems announce. Boswell is very much aware of the landscape of sound and emotional separation which good poetry deals with at crunch time, the verbal body perfectly tuned into what pushes the mind upwards or downwards, or not at all.

In the poem "Diminuendo" we get this:

> the world's non sequiturs
> return flushed and breathless
> prodigal hecklers who've
> walked miles of unmown
> fields sleeping children
> slung across their backs

And we also get this:

> the river glinting below us
> wind & sun drying the land's
> comely face after last night's
> storm shook the spirit free

And, finally, there are these lines from the title poem "Some Far Country:"

> dark sacred morning
> rain barrel filled to the brim
> mirror-black surface
> belies another life below
>
> things as they are
> without question or reason
> no string or Cartesian
> theory here is the hand
> you're dealt now play it
> here is the shape of the cloud
> now color it in

Ifeanyi Menkiti
February 2013

For Polly

everything that happens
will happen today
　　　—David Byrne

Oliver's Prologue

His sly smile like his older brother's
not entirely innocent. We have
trouble with goodbye—far simpler
to insult the heart's status quo

let someone else feel the draft and
close that door. The way your parents
lovingly chainsawed the furniture with
their vitriolics those months before

they sent you off to school, the house
a war zone after dad flipped the car
driving home from yet another
assignation and kept right on

commuting to & from his other life,
all so you could take the scissors and
neatly cut the cord with your own hand.
Or the knife of unconditional trust your

protégé used to stab you in the back,
enabling you to torch the remains of
a job you loved and needed to leave.
Or how the distance grew with her

premonitions, forswearing mud pies
and platitudes, a simple kiss behind
the ear deaf already to birdsong eyes
blind to children liberating the yard

the long walk begun from her favorite
porch into the dusky field beyond.
There are no words for it. Sometimes
you need to stop going and be gone.

Forgotten even if forgiveness is
not an option. We both know Judas
didn't give a shit about the silver.
So don't take it personally should

his brother teach him to call
people bridges and ask if they
have a lasso, knowing full well
he has trouble with his 'R's & 'L's

which some may find amusing or
even endearing sung from a three
year-old's mouth. Or not. Either way
the river runs rogue as a rodeo when

I say to you my own dear reader
you are both a lasso to be slipped
and a bridge to be crossed then burned
like the page you must now turn.

SOME FAR COUNTRY

*I will go off to some far country
Where I'll know no one and no one knows me.*

—Kate Rusby

Iceman

Stars receive us more dimly
because of how we have behaved.
You said there would be repercussions:
no more electricity or running water,

but this is less than I am used to.
The refrigerator so bare it echoes.
Condiments don't count, except maybe
olives, jewels of Aegean sun trapped

in jars. The freezer is another story.
It coughs and rattles all night,
crystallizing a lump of cryogenic fossils.
Is it any coincidence I feel like

the Iceman of Hauslabjoch, staring out
through inches of glacier at your squinted
face drenched in kitchen light. My pouch
of bones preserved, perfectly intact, wasted.

Repairmen can conjecture as long
as they want. No one will ever
guess how I perished beside the frozen
peas, before my time, while hunting.

The Patience of Roméo Dallaire

While someone else is eating or opening a window or just
walking dully along...
—from "Musée des Beaux Arts" by W. H. Auden

Cherry blossoms along the river bank deign to be admired.
The tongue inside the knife inside the fruit inside the flower.

Months in stasis quibbling over a definition. How many
hacks of one boy's ax before a tree falls at his father's feet.

For him, was it not an important failure? A taste will tease
more than appease an appetite. The graves are not yet quite full...

the ploughman lends a hand, marvels at his own efficiency.
You wonder how Brueghel might have rendered, or would he too

have turned away quite leisurely to capture a more stomachable
scene of everyday misfits and imbeciles conducting the usual

drunken indecencies with animals and farm implements? Who
is going to do the good work and help us fill them completely?

Miles up, Landsat mosaics map an opaque picnic—microbial tribes
of ants and roaches vie invisible beneath a cool, green canopy.

Our mouths are not yet quite full. A small fan bites into his
first ballpark frank as the Marlins lose to the Dodgers, 2 – 3.

Kansas State University police auction bicycles impounded
as abandoned property. OJ schemes how he'll get away with it,

hires a moonless night to hide his gloved hands. But for the blood-
flecked flamboyant, macaques nap unnoticed in afternoon perches.

Brown and inscrutable, the bloated river drags through scumbled
fields as if somewhere else something more human is happening.

Elsewhere, a bootless soldier curled under a park bench in Ottawa
seeks solace in the transubstantiation of olives and martinis,

unblinking cipher appointed to count without speaking, the eyes—
accusing, damning, imploring—so the rest can continue snoring.

—April 1994

And Pigs May Fly

—for Michael Hayes

I'm boarding my flight home from the heartland,
overflowing with hope for humanity and grace of good
people I've met, when the red-cheeked man in front of me
tries to stuff his oversized duffel into an overhead bin.
Unremarkable in itself, except the crumpling resistance
he's experiencing belongs to the couple beside me—
their garment bag with wedding clothes now being
squashed to the size of a shriveled carnation. Rather
than seek the nearly empty compartment next to theirs,
he removes the couple's bag and hands it to them,
saying it sure would help him out. Incredulous, she lays
their wardrobe's wrinkled remains under the seat in front of her.
Not as if this is a big flight either, where individual motives and
ordinary desperation can skulk in a stuffed tin turkey of nerves:
just a crop hopper between Columbus and Cleveland.
Airborne, I gaze at the farmers' neat patchwork where once
Shawnee sat on bare ground expecting an apology
and got the opposite from Mad Anthony Wayne. What will
it take I wonder—a heart attack, losing someone close—
to bring the minutiae miles below into focus, for him
to reach for his rip cord and realize he's chute-less
with the ground coming up fast.
"I'm just lookin at gate numbers to see where I gotta go,"
he announces to no one in particular as we taxi to the terminal,
as if his were the sole connection, our reason for traveling—
to keep him company and his airfare low, smile at his impunity
the way one regards a basket of severed hands of Congolese
rubber slaves. I unbuckle and haul my own carryon out
from under his seat, the dry aftertaste of contrition like salted
nuts on my silent tongue. Why didn't I speak up? I could have
said something, or from my vantage plagued him for forty-five
minutes, imitating with the tip of my pen a reconnoitering fly
landing on the white heliport of his head. At the very least
I could have winked—a mute solidarity for the woman
next to me and her husband who, seconds before the cabin
door opens, whips out a *Playboy* and begins reading.

Truth

yes my love
we all lie
because we don't know any better
or worse
because we can't tell a limo
from a hearse
or vow from a curse
or even what's coming
in the next verse

come here she said
look me in the eye
and say that

Mirror

I had an errand to do
away from your bed
had to refill your scripts
get you your meds
I straightened my hair in
the mirror you scowled
Vanity was all you said

Proviso

world you bid us
come seek & find
admire & praise if
your heart can take it
all in and learn to
let it all go again

Mangrove

But he could see everyone on the beach
was on vacation, that each wished to escape
for a while, maybe forever, all the great questions.
—from "Dostoyevsky in Wildwood" by Stephen Dunn

Glass towers glint vainglorious,
    rise overnight in flight paths of cranes—
        hammock and bleached oyster mounds

now a Cadillac ranch of cruise ships
    sunken prow-first in shrinking sand lots
        with names heisted from Riviera towns,

a necklace of concrete and steel
    spooled around the wetlands' throat,
        choking light, air, water . . .

[handwritten: — critical]

all that moves within fakahatchee grass,
    splayed tufts of saw palmetto and
        sea grape giving way to charred

bone-yard of black mangrove. Roach-sized
    crabs skitter among roots, retreat in concentric
        ripples down sand pores the way so-called

friends stop talking the moment
    you enter a room, the air unnaturally dead,
        warm and humming with what wasn't said.

Three ibis pick through tannic peat,
    ghostly stiltwalkers stepping gingerly
        among *pneumatophores*—a word

that keeps resurfacing ever since
    our tram driver drawled it offhand
        one trip down the boardwalk.

I took him for a retired English professor—
        explaining how we, like the clever trees,
                must learn to breathe by other means

when humanity's meconium smothers
        roots and stunts our growth, and how
                when Narcissus is found face down

in a tidal pool beside the roseate spoonbill,
        we'll look to others whose resemblance,
                despite odd feathers and scales,

suggests a truth unguessed till now—
        before grasping the homonomy of his Greek.
                We linger at the beach, drinking with

morbid fascination our final sangria
        catharsis, forbidden passage past
                the sponge of swamp that separates sea

from city like a gate between Eden and Gomorrah.
        I forego my professor's tram ride, skirting
                the demarcation between grove and man.

Seems it always ends this way: returning alone
        through tangled trees in slanted light, family gone
                on ahead, willing pack mule of towels and

sand-caked toys, sandal slap of boardwalk slats
        absorbed by the low canopy. Vacation's headlong
                extinction slows. Joy-ride cyclists coast past,

clock hands of crank arms backpedaling
        in gearless insouciance. I pause at intervals
                and let the trees breathe for me.

Calico spiders stretch like dark stars
        between branches, motionless sentinels
                of another galaxy. Back through salt-

tolerant *avicennia germinans*, black stands
   bee-keepers favor, setting out hives in early
      summer for their abundant flowers;

past *rhizophura mangle* whose aerial roots
   walk with me, their glossy propagules, dangling
      genitalia fully germinated and ready;

brackish smell dissipating, white trunks
   of *laguncularia racemosa* silent as gravestones.
      Corrugated flanks of sun drunk gators

long gone from lagoon banks. Only
   an egret's stasis interrupts the half-
      light's departure, while we slip

into quicksand, over our heads in seconds,
   mud sealing every pore, outstretched fingers
      rooting for the familiar kiss of a new life.

Woman who hates jazz nevertheless

digs my no-holds barred pugilism
with the avant garde a drummer's
agon alternately feathering high hats
& taiko-flailing toms two-fisted
his bipolar throne a paragon gone

mild mid the singer's throaty gaslamp
poured like gravy over synapses,
more apt to bifurcate kamikazes
at the bar than spell relief to sparring
partners double-hung in forget-me-not

blouses, catatonic matrons in back numb-
ering rifles. "Let's hear one on the black
keys only!" the scuppernong shouts his rib
eye appalling while the horn & reed do
their business in nobody else's garden go

fumbling in the larder for a modicum of
laudanum, pass synecdoches of sound
around the smokesweet room as if
lamenting chops long gone, each one
kissing the ass of his predecessor's riff

"Can the panegyrics, this number ain't
no abacus!" pure response—no call—
he's all serene marbles impoverished
by professors' tongues, leans into each
phrase contumely cat scat transfig-

urations language staggers through
subterranean stations abandoned
but for a final tremolo the open
instrument case everyone else walks
past on their free ride to redemption

the narrator
is the only one
who cares
about jazz

I would love to
hear this aloud

Found

The sculptor explains what we're looking at
is actually a piece of art. (side view of a video
monitor) *You'll see what I mean when I show you
the front.* (click) There, burnt into the screen's pixels,
ghosts the faint afterimage of a hallway or lobby
like any you might find in a hotel or condominium—
blank walls, glass doors, two-toned diamond carpet.
Is it turned off? one woman wants to know. Yes,
he repeats, clicking back to the previous slide,
pointing out the exempt cathode tube, the flaccid
plug. *What medium is it?* one artist wisecracks.
We stare some more at the monitor's screen
the way its camera stared at the same dull scene
for fifteen years, and listen to the sculptor describe
in technical terms how the rendering mimics
a palimpsest or early daguerreotype in its expression,
trying to convince us what he found in a sidewalk
dumpster is a seminal creation, and not a fluke
of technology headed for a landfill on Staten Island.
Would his case be stronger if we detected
the spectral movements of residents who lived
there, the quotidian contrails of their transitory
to's and fro's? Or if he'd painted figures on the glass,
say, a doorman, an old woman and her Pekinese?
Would we then see art, not as something worth salvaging
but as our salvation? (And why are we spending more
time on this one slide than all his others combined?)
Or would it be better—for the same reason
the *Giro d'Italia* isn't staged on bike paths and
real farmers slaughter and eat their own animals—
if he'd kept his dirty little discovery to himself?

16

Game Night at Fenway

I fall asleep beside you in the back of the ambulance
the closest we've slept in weeks meds carrying you off

on a journey within a journey I wonder are you as
disoriented upon waking from the same shared dream

to a nightmare traffic jam inching into the maw of that
mortal city your frail fate in the hands of two novice

EMTs a world away from rural Vermont so young
& uncertain how to find our final destination relying

blindly on their GPS directing them to a parking lot
behind Yawkey Way on game night streets choked with

die-hard fans here to pull their team from a losing streak
its biggest dive in decades a statistic impossibly far

from where you lay win / lose it's all the same you'd say
the driver and his sidekick about to wet their pants more

panicked than their passengers at the prospect of being lost
boy soldiers entering battle for the first time paralyzed by

the tide of all that humanity their errand one prolonged
pulse of emergency it's okay I assure them we've been

here before we know the way and he turns off the computer
to let a human voice get us out of this mess

to Boston, to the illness

Blues for M'Baïki

—for Scott Campbell

Tati will have none of my clandestine
Lomaxing: *Nous allons*…she takes
my hand, leads me inches from her neighbor's
firelit yard. I hesitate and hang back;

I didn't know the dead girl,
only her boyfriend.
And wouldn't her family find my moony
whiteness—microphone in hand—

another roué uncle sowing a virus he hid?
What did I know of death, or any gram
of that place but periphery—the spaces
between beats I wanted to steal and cram

into my backpack? All night, rhythms
summon the unseen, folding a prayer
from one stretched skin to another.
I resist the tainted fête, the way her

teeth tease, bright as dried cassava.
Through the gaping silence since
friends and family slip—still, the tape
loops forward and back: Tati's

eager laughter, my contrition mixed
with muffled voices of the grieving,
a drummer's layered polysemies of sound
pummeling us to sleep like surf, leaving

mute eulogies for a wrack of people who
measure time by heartbeats not clocks.
We grope through wood smoke and bushes,
loath to crash a party that never stops.

[handwritten marginalia: tourism]

[handwritten marginalia: Can Americans understand death the way the people in other countries do?]

Midsummer Dance

—after Anders Zorn

Understanding, bittersweet and fleeting,
complete in its singular contraction—
a glimpse of fireweed by the roadside.
A bell in the village square that hasn't rung
in centuries, blown to song by a rogue
gust. A maypole mistaken centuries later
for a railroad crossing. Ashes of unused sin
scattered beneath poplars, silver herring
shimmer in schools of false light.

Couples of Dalarna, curfewless leaves
swept by cyclones of song, drunk on daylight
sunken to a shallow depth, costumed as if fated
for each other, as if earth herself gave consent.
Fiddle and accordion saw and scissor the dusky
farmyard, racing ahead, urgent and undulant;
blurred bodies keep pace, quicken in hypnotic
centrifuge, bruised smell of grass tamped
by lightsome feet—requiting the marathon
winter in a single seamless summer day

when hay is made in the grained-light midnight,
raked and sheafed, stealing time's onward sweep
like the dervish who divines the still center
of self-orbit. Sunrise reflected in upper windows
of the red house behind them and in faces possessed,
souls whirling, lost—tomorrow already upon them,
whole rye fields bartered for an unmade bed,
hats and bonnets, shirtsleeves and skirts
loosening, and from their flying sweat-
soaked garments, a wind.

Wonder

There was not even any sound, because of the sand.
—Antoine de Saint-Exupéry

the night before the day you stared god in the eye
and god blinked you became the clock we watched
your hours condensed to a holiness of breath deep
in cavernous sleep…or so we assume until you hear
his playing from another room and cock your head
and your own mother goes to ask him to *come in and
play for your mother I think she likes it* and he comes
and sits beside your bed and strums and sings
a Natalie Merchant song he learned your oldest son
who graduates from high school next year while your
youngest little prince dreams in another room he
has all the stars laughing only for him the rhythm
of blood a perpetual tune in his chest as your own
rises and falls a leaky raft at sea and you drift far from
everything you'll miss in their lives far from anything
resembling pity or regret eyes closed resigned to never
sighting land again you listen with the faintest smile
on your lips to this strange wondrous music which
seems to be flowing from somewhere deep inside
of you as the shy boy you always liked but never
spoke to approaches and asks you for this dance

beautiful

After Two Lines Simultaneously Nearing the End of Books by Jean Valentine and Jane Austen

Do you remember, last time
we saw each other, how the first thing
led to the next, my head lost
in a novel, yours in a poem—
our ideas of love orbiting in opposite
directions. A roulette ball of pure
silver, a blurred wheel of fire.

Conflict

Or city gardens in winter
hemmed by wrought iron
—holly, rhododendron, azalea—
their fulgent leaves green flames
against snow, hallucinogenic islands,
Shangri las of defiance engulfed
by your deciduous indifference.

Do you remember my mouth
black & blue from what I said
—gaffe, faux pas, malaprop—
all French to you and Greek

to my 4/4 rhyme. You stood in the doorway
& listened to the church bell chime—
as usual my timing sucked. I wanted you
to fly the day the planes all crashed.

*ouch—
angry—
bitter*

*a little
too vague
for me. the Title reference
is lost on me*

Saltimbanques

the circus has left town
and moved on

we loiter here
on a barren plain
costumed in
the hues you chose

wondering what to do
now that our big top
is gone

end of relationship (previous poem).

the slightest gesture
and we begin again

to move the way
our limbs were
trained to move

to perform for ourselves

isn't this what
we've always done?

Nice
the simplicity
works here

Distances

Travelling at night so our engine wouldn't overheat
we ran out of gas in a one-bar town in central Idaho

although now I've noticed the preceding two lines
are precisely the same length, not approximately but

abruptly at the end of a fenced stretch of military land
we emerged from the car like chrysalides after a week

identically parallel as twin chromosomes holed up in
pine-knotted kabins or kottages, driving me mad one

fermented in a rank vat, two car-camping college kids
devoid of personal hygiene, the air there was splendid

moment with imprecision, refreshing the way those last
two came together, I couldn't have planned it better how

the barkeep (an off-duty sheriff) spared us a gallon or
two in the moon-shade of a great cottonwood outside

the bar contained in estimation fifty characters more or
less. Maps made it nearly impossible to exact exactitude

in that one-bar town with the perfect air, if not for the
sweet man behind the counter who was willing to stop

measuring with a busted odometer the right distance
from nowhere, we could just as easily have ended up

pouring drinks long enough to put our mephitic young
carcasses back on the road again. Or we could have run

out of fuel there with everyone home in bed and
found that where we arrived was where we were.

The Weather in Karbala

Twenty-five below—the car thermometer informs us
with digital indifference on our way to school. Not the minus
hundred-twenty-five atop Mount Washington, still, the ink in this pen
frozen like pre-perestroikan veins of marble, sealed in a statue in Murmansk.

Column of white smoke rising from the distant schoolhouse into clear value-
neutral sky, free of association, monotonic as public radio underwriting
not out to sell a thing. We file past toppled idols. Trees and
mailboxes, standing seams rimed with hoarfrost,

moonscape of valley floor shrouded from the low
ineffectual sun that may as well be another star or edelweiss
bloomed from stone, a five-year-old artist's aesthetic touch, added
as an afterthought to make the day more realistic. Even parents adamant

about hats & mittens appear to have won this morning. Bundled forms,
small and purposeful, scurry toward front doors as if wombward,
boots squeaking across packed snow, eyes watering, pinched
nostrils siphoning the waxen air. Stay warm, we used

to say weeks ago—gratefully escaping parkas,
peeling layers of wool and polypropylene at classroom
cubbies, melting into the routine warmth of friends and your
Kindergarten teacher's voice as if aggression were only a history lesson

collecting shelf dust in a dead primer. Before the snap bent and bite swallowed
us whole, back when sarcasm worked and rhetoric warmed our insides
like a stiff Scotch. Before mothering meteorologists admonished
don't go outside unless you have to. Before we covered

hope with the balaclava of dream and could stand
shivering in doorways able to talk about
the weather, able to really say what
was on everyone's mind.

Are You My Boo Radley?

the shining piece of tinfoil
in the knothole of a maple

remind me how good this feels
you sighed the last time
we made love

corn chest-high now
fixed on the rise & fall of each breath
incredulous a summer so young
and lush will take its last

I see you've gone to paperback
pretty soon to kindle
to ether

here where clocks have been known
to repeat a generation
or slip into reverse
where car horns are removed
at birth

where friends are hard to come by
and harder to keep

where we put all our eggs
in the basket of family
& bung them about from barn
to house trusting one won't fall out

delphinium phlox coneflower sage
reds purples pinks & whites
of our slowly drying eyes

colors subdued now by late
summer's wave of wild volunteers
milkweed goldenrod Queen Anne's lace
same as every year we disappear
into a sea of meadow

until there is no difference
the blur between the work of wind and birds
and what someone's hands planted

the earth we inhabit and
the one that inhabits us

above the riot
ethereal wisps of tiny violet
flowers with no name sway
anorexic on lithe stems
attenuating to sky

weightlessness of childhood
too soon too fast
gone to seed
gone by
gone

The Mission

Oh yeh, yeh man, she de one luv, dat lil girl.
*She what keep me going…*he lisps through a train
wreck of teeth, tattered dreads gnarled up in the hood
of his frayed army surplus parka. We stand toe to toe,
swaddled by the savory flatulence of all-nite delis,
fumbling with a faded, wrinkled Polaroid. That he
may not know its subject misses the point.
We mumble and nod under the hotel's heat lamps
as if between the two of us we've seen it all—
until our lies become their own accompaniment.
You need some help, sir? the doorman interrupts.
(*Can't you see he does?* I want to say.) Our collars
turned against an arctic furnace of wind whipping
down Seventh Avenue. I hand him what's left,
whatever the debauch didn't take. Tomorrow
I'll walk past him as if he were less than a shadow,
a crack in the sidewalk. But tonight we hug,
two more covert operatives waiting for a rescue
chopper that never comes to lift us from the first grains
of dawn's infantry, slinking around the corner of 53rd
the hangover already begun.

Drunk — helping the homeless?

Good one — a story here

The Documentarists

Welcome to Sierra Leone.
If you cannot help us,
please do not corrupt us.
  —billboard at Freetown airport, Sierra Leone

The young Americans were careful
to introduce themselves as fellow musicians,
not journalists or filmmakers. It was critical
to patronize themselves first and ask questions later.
Imperative to implement the trick of distracting
ubiquitous swarms of small children from
the foreground of every frame with soccer balls
& Frisbees. Essential at length to adopt
the patient resignation of their dispossessed
subjects, war-torn from their homes and broken
down on a backroad to Babylon, who apologize
after conferring in private—
We are sorry but we have no dramas.
Above all fundamental to let woodsmoke cloud
every motive for why they'd come, to accept
without hesitation from a makeshift shred of less
than nothing each & every courtesy offered:
to stay up too late drinking palm wine & whiskey,
singing & playing in a place where music, in theory,
should not exist; to eat the same chicken & manioc
with their hands from the same black pot, or silence
thirst's cicada from the same cistern; receive shelter
in a tarpaulin house (too hot), sleep on a tarpaulin mat
(too cold) long enough to divest thread counts &
the familiar template of loved ones now waking
half a world away above a bay of fog

before Mohammed could sit down and say
how the cutlass grazed his eye and exposed
his skull; how with the good one left he saw
his parents cut down with a violence
so indiscriminate their killer vanished
leaving only the weapon's arc in air;
how the soldiers' drunken taunts & laughter

could have been mistaken from the street
for a holiday party; how neighbors' accounts
of treachery could not have prepared him
for how casually the invisible one
promised he would be next
if he did not place his child in a pestle
and pound the life from him with a mortar
and feel grateful when they cut off his hand
to forever remind him of his transgression.
Calmly adding his own commentary
to a drama he would freely give
someone else if he could,
I will never return to that place
as if the camera wasn't there.

Beautiful -
Stunning and sad
- Americans onll
again exploiting
Africa

Just Remember I Knew You When

Prime example I'm apt to cite is Lenny,
who forked his mind's manure for years
caretaking that north-sloping, hill-hunched
farm while chasing down a MFA as if it were

a cagey ewe, so he could justify the hours
between feedings and mending fences.
Shelved screenplays stacked like haybales
in disheveled abandon beside an enormous

cookie jar of pennies, one saved for every
stagnant phrase exhumed and dragged
from the tomb of process. Every dispensation
of hayleaf and grain, he'd dream of stuffing

that wadding into his hometown's canon,
waiting for the fuse to catch, the flint to knock
smartly against the frizzen making sparks,
the charge to leap into the barrel, followed

at length by distant bursting. Who could say
how far its arc might reach, what town
might wake and think fireworks or lightning?
And when lo at last the powder did ignite

you could see it in his eyes. A Hollywood
contract, front page of the local weekly,
daily calls from an agent whose sun-drenched
assurances and mineral water excuses blurred

whatever artificial differential once existed
between coasts. Could he hear his own
lightly dredged laughter at parties, cynical
lemon twist of luck he wished a recent graduate

brave enough to admit she was trying her uncallused
hand at short fiction? Could he taste the gelignite
of early fame rising in the back of his throat,
his saliva now an appraised thing?

The month on the lot, holding more strings
than a director, actors turning in their mouths
the fruit from his own backyard trees,
asking permission to pick & eat. Rumors inflate

like Macy's balloons till we figure, well, that's
the last this shrunken pond will see of him . . .
but then he's filling up at the pump,
looking the same old sheenless penny

as if he'd never left, no guy ropes dangling
like dreadlocks from his head. So, I ask,
when are we going to see that world premiere
at the Town Hall? *Oh that*, he sneers,

I wouldn't let my own daughter watch that shit
and climbs in his truck. We wait a year or so
and finally forget before unearthing it
in the action-adventure racks of a big city

video store. A sci-fi western about prospecting
for gold on another planet, maybe you've seen it:
the marvelously abundant myriad of expletives
available to every life form, the sample of each

character's persona maculate to the core.
We endured for twenty hard fought minutes
before giving up. You know it's bad when your
fiancée says nudity would have improved it.

His daughter's in high school now. He manages
his father's lumberyard where at least there's
an identifiable smell, the whine of saws
biting into something that once grew.

Still

just when I think you
have vanished for good
dissolved into the radiance

of our children
you come again
in those drifting
forsaken hours
it may only be

a small cameo you play
a chinwag over dinner
or tip on laundry soap
a short visit just
dropping by to say
hi I'm still here
& so are you

then again every role
pales beside your final
command performance
for which there are no
awards or published reviews
only word-of-closed-mouth
only wind in the trees

Stalin recorded a half-
hour ovation for himself
(his audience assumed
the first to cease clapping
would win a one-way
ticket to the gulag)

we gather and sit
in silence on your hill
this is how much
we love you still

Guard Duty

...late, so late, even the moon
has lost its voice, off the deep
end of dreamtime and yet,
a light still on downstairs
as if the ceiling and floor
separating us glowed with your burning,
as if I, the resident somnambulist
in superhero jammies, trolling
the dark waters of our house,
half-expected to find you there,
scratching your head at the kitchen
counter or passed out on the couch
in a haze of cigar smoke,
spooked by the ninja stealth
of the Japanese soldier who snuck
down from his cave the night you
were on guard duty (*to sabotage
the airbase* you said). *Halt! Who
goes ther*e? you ordered and
fired a potshot into the jungle—
your reply when asked if you ever
killed anyone in combat.
But it was just me, nomad
in a nocturnal no man's land,
willingly led by the unseen hand
of my mind's eye. I'd strike up
a philosophical dissertation on
our dog, or some daily trauma
from second grade...
and you'd play along, talking me
down, rehearsing for those nights
I'll come home with a buzz on
to find you up waiting—shooting the
subtext the way sons and fathers might—
till you asked wouldn't I rather be in bed
and the bottom dropped out.
Glazed, rhetorical, abruptly self-conscious
of the minefield around us—*I'm sleep-
walking again aren't* I...and you left

your post to guide me through the maze
of hallways and stairs my dreams
echolocated eons ago,
back to the far reach of an
unstrategic island, our footsteps
erased behind us by the tide
like a treaty's best intentions
over time.

The Deep End

—for Thomas Lux

I can't help wonder if Doug—the boy who strafed
our sisters with water balloons from his bedroom window
and introduced us to the quarries at Pigeon Cove: heights
so counterintuitive, not even sneakers could mute the sick

smack of a misjudged entry—ever let it all ride
before a dive in the shallow end of a neighbor's pool
ended the betting for him. Or whether he feels lucky
to leave with pocket change, the grand prize winner

of a single centimeter missed by the dealer's rake.
Seeing him strapped to his chair that summer after,
staring from his porch at the breakers we body surfed
just last year, one finds it hard to loll on the beach

and burn, to feel safe in our skin and not question
the tidal rocks we never thought twice about leaping from,
harder still to take the moon seriously again with its
mezzanine of stars listening, overwhelmed with longing.

You have to hope the boy never tasted the liquor of another's
lips. That he was somehow spared. But knowing Doug
he's upped the ante long after the house has folded,
practicing on the back of a hand he can now raise by himself.

The Parade

always someone else getting to ride
flaunt decorum in the first pew
drum and trumpet in full view
testify without having to lie

in a rum punch gutter off Saint Peter's
borne next morning umbrella high
on savory waves of beignets and chicory
by old jazz men in ties and boaters

as doves alight on black iron balconies
and hosed down streets begin to shine
the way we wriggled & writhed at my
Great Aunt Eula's obsequies

knowing she would have smiled
and shouted hallelujah lifting up
our eyes instead of mumbling cups
of knee dust by rote getting riled

and ourselves some lovin in between
like Langston wrote beating bushes
sure as gumbo chases sin the child rushes
in to question why the end comes pristine

when up to that point goes anything but
sure as parents fear the child misbehaves
silence his jungle gym of empty staves
played all night by saints who hang a right

at Ursulines & bury me in air so I won't
float when the waters rise sealed in stone
but leave the window open...
I don't want to miss a note

Variations on a Toy Xylophone

every nine minutes
the world stops ticking

I ask the same question
in a different way

every nine minutes
the flame in my heart

flickers higher as if
the palm of your hand

has brushed against mine
inadvertently or maybe

every nine minutes the beetle
squirming on its back

rights itself to a new
possibility your hour

comes not when you are
most free but when you

are most needed who is this
loony who parks & sits in his

car awaiting further instructions?
solipsists roam & roam

looking for a likely backwater
to colonize & claim their own

every nine minutes the wind
shifts revealing the conscience

of trees the only super power
that appeals at the moment:

invisibility: to be here
without being here: buried

in a pile of leaves every nine
minutes you call with another

question I can't answer you
find yourself in the weeds again

swinging away with your dull
machete not so much to

navigate a way in or out
as to locate a prayer you once

wore around your neck but lost
before you knew it was more

than a symbol and these dreams
are more than just dreams

Dinner with Uncle Tom

—for Charles Baker

The oak-dim sports bar smelled like a warm, oiled glove.
We sat and watched you devour a steak and fries, one game away
from three hundred wins, palming us with annals of your day job—
management's shufflings of lesser deities, to you mere names in a cap
scrambling from town to town, Triple-A to front office, scrounging
for better stats—a paunchy, middle-aged businessman, hardly
the center of Fenway's universe we lionized from the wives' box
behind home plate, her breath still held on every pitch after
all these years. You picked your teeth and laughed so the whole
place could overhear, as if it were child's play to hum a calf-
skinned ball past kids half your age. *Always carry a pitchfork
into the bullpen* you aphorized between bites, sharing the secret
of your longevity: how you put your whole body behind every
knuckle, curve and slider, unlike the doomed arms of young
speedballers—the same holistic approach you were using
to segue smoothly from diamond to lecture circuit,
the facile grace of your half-full mouth conducting our roundtable
as if you were still on the mound, retiring vignettes like batters,
then sending the ball around the horn to make sure everyone—
even the youngest nephew—touched it at least once.
A year past college, narcissistic gods downsizing all around us,
little league uniforms long mothballed, no more easy signals
from a catcher's crotch: how could we hope for a perfect game
with dead beat dad stealing home next door, when a bunt or pop
fly could seal our fate, the replay button stuck on Billy Buckner's
bowlegs; the game, now a series of balks and wild pitches rushing in
to fill a void of legends behind glass cases—empty reliquaries
of husbands and fathers, grown men scarfing what they can
scare up at this late hour, while we watch having already eaten.

How This Next Song Came To Be

We forgive the folksinger for tuning her guitar half the night.
It buys her time to loosen up the crowd with a routine so candid
you can't tell whether the talk is for the tuning's sake or a form of therapy.

It doesn't matter; we end up loving her—both the persona behind
a microphone and the woman her music infers. How cleverly
she effaces herself as if she's one of us! Tweaking her

low E peg while evoking her baby daughter like a surgeon calibrating
our inner harmonic, her deft fingers plying the open cavity.
Jokes, cheap arpeggios, a disarming blend of pathos

and cynicism—the audience politely endures a playlist
of excuses. We don't even mind when her strings flat & sharp
as she points out our spiritual blemishes—everyone knows the song

will come and all else will be pardoned. Compliant as the Jonestown
elect we savor every drop and marvel how spotlights ricochet
off her instrument's inlay and chrome, chasing iridescent

unplayed notes into the sea of seats where impassive stones
roll in & out helpless before each wave, reverberating to a smooth
polish our endless scales, practiced for no one with no promise of a tune,

carried by the exhale of her encore an ocean away from those populated
shores where the evening started, we float through open
doors into night's pelagic, deaf embrace.

Our Little Japes

The trouble with children is you can't return them—Quentin Crisp

A couple cars ahead, a male pedestrian is scurrying across
the main drag into town during AM rush hour headed for
the daycare across the street with a coffee in one hand and his
child in the other. But he's having trouble juggling both while

mixing the metaphor of his morning, the coffee's slipping
and now, with vehicles alternately yielding & whizzing
by him at indignant rates of speed, he has to make a choice:
my son or my coffee?

And I'm reminded of when our first child was born,
my wife made a point of relating, among other new parent
horror stories, the one about the new dad who was supposed
to drop his little angel no more than a few months old

off at day care, but being new at the job, he drives instead
out of habit to his office as he maps out the day's itinerary
like a power point presentation in his head, and pleased
with himself to have arrived early enough to park only

a few spaces removed from his usual lucky spot, goes about
the morning's business fighting to find that I-need-more-coffee-
it-must-be-Tuesday groove until around noon when his wife
calls to ask how the drop off went and how their little darling

seemed with the day care provider and whether he remembered
to tell them about the funky new nipple on the bottle, at which
point she hears the receiver drop followed by several minutes
of uniform silence save for the intermittent sotto voce of Carl

in the neighboring cubicle badmouthing mutual funds while
advertising his golf handicap, and what with temperatures
already in the nineties that day and the windows up, well,
we need not dwell on this guy's future as a father, how much

effort it takes to water a seed, to weed now & then, and even if
it turns out in its mid-teens to be nothing but weed, stubborn,
invasive & pernicious as the surly disavowed bracken you
yourself surely were, wouldn't something wild in you still

want to coax it along its firebombed road to world domination?
Is he to blame for being born like most men with an intuitive
repertoire the size of a pinto bean that vacillates between stomach
and groin. We deem his soul unfit to change a diaper, but beyond this

experts disagree. Should there be a special prison for bad parents where
they're forced to juggle coddling orphaned crack babies 24/7 and splinting
limbs of injured birds and rodents, before they have a prayer for parole—
for all the belt-wielding misopedians & bottom-feeding ferberizing

bottom-bruisers, the must-finish-your-peas-before-you're-excused-from-
the-tablers, benign neglecters whose FPS-obsessed son can't distinguish
between vector graphics and the dead bodies of his classmates, the vicarious
butt-lipped throat-screamers slinging insults at six year old ball players?

And what of the parents of "James Holley, age 16, last seen at 7:30 AM
on February 28 wearing a green and red kilt, blue polo shirt and brown
hiking shoes with light brown laces"…who inadvertently advertised his
suicide by posting a picture of their missing son in every store front for

fifty miles? Can we blame them too for misplacing their no longer wee
bairn, Moses in the bullrushes, Huang Xi forgotten in the huotong while
a carved boy rides a qilin above her parents' bed to help them conceive a
sacred son destined for high officialdom? Supposing you're eighteen &

socially inept and just arrived in Vienna where your roommate and you
are assigned to a flat whose only bathtub is located in the family kitchen
and whose Hausfrau has a new baby who keeps you up most of the night,
and when his Mutter who needs the rent hears you might be moving

to another less domestic living situation (because you came to Europe
this semester *to get away from* your family) redoubles her efforts between
feedings and classes to teach you the German language—sits you down
for a whirlwind tour of their Küchen pointing at (repeat after me)

der Eisschrank, Salz, Pfeffer, der Tiegel, das Mehl, die Eier, der Zucker…
imploring you in broken English through hormonal post-partum tears
please to must no leave because they desperately need the rent, and you reassuring
her everything will be fine knowing full well you and Ernie are out of there

first thing in the Morgen before Frühstück without so much as an Auf
Viedersehen und Danke Viemals und Viel Glück with little Adolph
and that sleep deprivation thing, without realizing she's not to blame
since children are a joke our parents play on us, which goosesteps

to a poem by a woman with the same surname, forename Louise,
who ventriloquized Circe to say "I never turned anyone into a pig./
Some people are pigs; I make them/Look like pigs…Your men weren't
bad men;/Undisciplined life/Did that to them"—astutely observing

that in the cosmology of male sentience, the planet Id is orbited not
by the moon Super-ego but by a super-sized mammary, and the massive
universe of one, the ego itself, only gains size and speed on its descent
from the womb, can't stop or shrink or change direction, sure as hell

can't crawl back in, until its rolling mass of collateral affliction has swept
a few infanticides and genocides along with it, because men are autotheistic
jehus & young ones especially who can get away with narcissistic volumes
and not even know when they're feisting and not fessing up because the world

is their beer-battered oyster and so what if you twist some panties, ruffle some
underage plumage, tell a friend she looks boyish after her hooterectomy…
the bar is full of second, third, fourth, fifth even sixth chances
all moaning like Sirens begging *Come to me, I don't care about your past*

then in the next breath, *Just don't fuck up my future.* But there's
no rope in my hand out here on this limb, and while it may
be mostly, it's never just yang or yin, meat or veg. We'll always be
in cahoots, Adolph und Eva up to their old tricks, taking turns

mooning us from the bunker, compulsively popping bubble wrap
baby boomers packed their unwanted wedding haul in like the great
lost art of Europe that no one misses, then, unimpressed in front
of the fitting room mirror saying *See, I told you I was as big as a house,*

devising ways to test that love: *Here Johnny, why don't you and Gloria
go play in that bank of poison ivy over there* and *maybe we* should *see other
people*, their cartoon selves passing back & forth the ticking bomb
in their hands: You *take it./No* you *take it./No really, I insist.*

Quiz

the little wren on the roof
outside our bedroom window
looks at the feeder then at me
turns and flies back into the snowy
air as if to ask how can this be
April? surely you're joking
and late April at that
when the doctor came in
that afternoon the last question
he asked after you could barely
tell him your name: What month
is it? the drab room vibrated
with your silence a simple
failure confirming the universe
outside stars continue to
fall covering seeds spilled
from an empty feeder
I can't tell you
whether it's night
or the shade between

In Hindsight, a Happy Accident

So this is what it boils down to—
a lobster pot of silent screams.

In your Dopp kit, a personal-size religion
of unrequited love you squeezed

from the top. A radio frequency
you dialed past, sure

you could find better reception,
a hipper playlist. Only to wistfully flip

back through blips of ad hype and
smarmy djs, as if the one island

of song in a static ocean can be found
with compass & coordinates. Why

should your torment differ
from Columbus lost in a landlocked

city in Ohio, or the telepathy
that shrinks the cell phone in your

palm to a pebble's still pond ripple,
echoing a simple mistake: my love,

come here. I need you.

Never the Twain

Perfect pearl suspended
  in the crosshairs of my apotheosis
    bright enough to read by

to do all the things
  you dreamed in daylight
    of doing but didn't dare

not with the sun there
  glaring you have to be-
    have under winged

surveillance unless yours is
  one badassed archangel
    in wayfarers pomaded

Memphis rebel you can't quite put
  your finger on something irresistible
    & not to be trusted in his johnnyroy-

elvisjerrylee swagger & Lansky's
  shirt gut-sure he'd sell you like
    Sam Phillips down the muddy

river for vinyl immortality &
  a stick of Beamans whereas mine
    all corporate merger mumbles

into his lapel perched like secret
  service on the U-haul building
    across the street talons

poised to pry me from the wreckage
  of another bombed out workday
    we soar between supermarket

& supper wired to children's
  babelsong our safe house
    roof now googlable from space—

remember that place? frozen
        sparks & shadowmime juxta-
                posed deep as artesian dreams

impervious to discovery
        or possession & therefore ruin
                in an hour maybe two

you'll return from your
        separate well-lit country
                after you've cleared their tables

collected tips I'll find wadded on
        the bathroom counter come morning
                the scent of last night's special

infused in your hair
        you won't mind if I don't wait up
                to watch this fallen

funambulist arc across
        summer's final panel
                the only clue to loss her

silent progress above the trees
        subtle bling of constellations
                dissolved in her domineering sheen

a gaudy surrogate backlighting
        a recurring dream in which
                we're both in the same place

at the same time
        wedded to a dark uncertain thrill
                before it dawned & became our life.

General Admission

Back in those days before he collaborated with every
pop wannabe that sauntered in and canned a video for MTV,
while he was still an icon-in-the-making, not a foregone
media-packaged, multi-formatted conclusion, back when
we like to think it was still about the music and people
came because they knew, not because it was the thing
to do, before they showed you what you were missing
on a screen the size of a house, and one man with a guitar
could be an orchestra, without effects for every conceivable
heaven-sigh and hell-cry choking the stage, and we were still
new at this and mostly volunteer and no one frisked you
and you could stroll from section to section unhassled
whether you had seats there or not and maybe by chance
run into someone you were hoping but not expecting to see
and you could walk together among the smiling disciples
just listening to the miracle pouring from a wall of speakers
as if from thin air, like a sweet wine you'd never tasted,
without having to say a word, without touching or even holding
hands, the light beginning to fade, the gingko and elm
enveloping the lawn with their long arms, the scent of tamped
grass and a joint being passed somewhere, not caring if you
had a seat or a job or even a way home, just being part of
that righteousness.

Santana

Making the Bed

This is not a life saving device.
—Aerobed warning label

a child floats in on morning's swell
and splashes about: *teach me to swim*
he insists *and I'll save you from drowning*

as easily as it inflated to cushion the blow
and separate us during nights & days
above & below those dark waters of

middle passage when no single vessel
could contain the pain I flip a switch
and suck out the air after all it was only

air and bodies crave solid things reverently
unfurl the sheets and tuck them between
the cherry frame a good friend carved at

the start of our life's voyage...nest of dream-
sweet conception of intimate matins &
restless nocturne novels & verse curled cats

& newborn babies snuggled tight now also
convalescence sickness & dying not a single
inch spared for euphemism...conveyance

across love's wordless water mooring from
which we drifted each night together and
apart always returning hand over hand

along the halyard home I recall the small
bed in the first room on the left in the
house across the street from Ford's

Theater where they set Lincoln adrift in
a coracle not his own and far too short
for his lanky frame and how essential

it was for you to be in this one place
ordained as if you could view infinity
from nowhere else the palliative team

scrambling to secure an ambulance
to get you here telling me you might
not endure the two-hour drive

how attendants angled your narrow
gurney upstairs and lay you in the open
field of your final crusade where once

you fought for victory now only for peace
surrounded by a galaxy of pillows and
the vivid nebula we draped across you

quilted by so many earnest hands
gathering lily lavender hyacinth every
bloom-warm harbinger inviting the ardor

of a spring that never came I tuck the deflated
mattress on a basement shelf and climb
in beside the light of your absence

Two Visits

I made you laugh after class
and you
you made me feel
a god among men
you are young
a new book I just picked up
and haven't read
with its perfect uncracked spine
and blank pages' endless fascination
yet to be filled then filled again
the idea of you inexhaustibly fresh
crossing the street arm in arm at the parade site
before the rally starts
all those other more handsome revolutionaries
the construction worker the UPS guy
I kiss your neck to remind them
to remind myself

~

you in the driver's seat
joking with the help with Peter R
dying's okay the old cat
sleeping near my head & me
letting her
you in the driver's seat
it's your bicycle you're trying to fix
smiling at me
eating tortellini soup
I offer you some but you're not hungry
Peter: if ever there was a reason for not
& we joking: we already used that one
it's okay you don't need to eat
no need to panic
you in the driver's seat joking with the help
slowly passing but forgoing
the country café
Peter are you skilled
at bike repair?

we can see clear through the clapboards
greeted by the young proprietor
of an old establishment
though weathered they do not age
I can help fix your bike I joke
rhetorical by now
you are in the driver's seat
I don't even know how to ride

Forty Words

I did not go into the meadow
did not steal through that
wide open window to lay
in tall grass or short grass
how can I say which grass
I did not get into that grass
at all

nor watch the milkweed rise
from our porch it wasn't anything
I could see beyond stonewall/
row of trees never stepped
through the gap there or
stood in the dying sun & took
my leave

it wasn't anything from where
I stood no sleight-hand of heaven
here on earth no slice of strawberry
rhubarb blueberry peach or any
other said with a sigh the wild
carrot knows too well the brush
of thigh

it never felt like summer at all
though we watched trees leaf
and melt into each other's green
grace don't let me tell you there
wasn't love there & plenty
not more than forty words from
this place

The New Paradigm

these first small weightless grains
of Bentley's obsession fall straight down

like a CPA's dust of numbers in mid-April
unpreoccupied with self or staging lyrics

in celebration of arriving at their final grassy
destination barely perceptible to naked

eye or skin know their strength is in numbers

in infinitely counting kin in density
& multiplicity no longer disavowed

among godwits who cram to fake
cleverness for clevernessake no more

marooned Crusoe making the most
of his assigned milieu its mute beauty

sticks and stays upon everything it touches
long after it's muffled shoveled or plowed

Reading

—for Katrina

attuned to the sound
wings make in white spaces

you wake in the middle
of a musical conversation

rapt in the padded thrall
of your cocoon's inner ear

eavesdropping on melodies
that unraveled as you slept

like the sweater you never
needed as much as the knitting

or the morning pool of floor light
that won't be shuttered or swept

glued to the sound
our dreams make in passing

along their sepia lit lanes
absent of billboards or dwellings

where the way grows fainter
and wild creatures prowl dense

thickets for the unsuspecting
victim who can tame them

August

the long awaited messenger finally
arrives in a month without mirrors
summer catches up with itself at last
content to chill in the pale gold heat
delight in bluetail damsels skimming
secrets on cellophane wings only
to lose them in cattails and duckgrass
sweet whispers unweave every dazed
leaf shimmering overtones of a lone

bell in the modest country
chapel where we married that
now sings for another pair who
fell in love yesterday morning
as if none ever tied the knot
there before or will again
and between each ring
a peal of children's laughter

from the nearby pond where
your childhood friends with young
families of their own flock like
egret wildebeest zebra lion gazelle
to the one watering hole for
miles around kids building aqueducts
& sand monuments to summer
capturing crayfish & painted
turtles in buckets zookeepers for
an afternoon heat-struck parties
swimming en masse to the raft

flotillas of inner tubes & waterwings
& bigger boys grappling & cannonballs
a headlong child wades her wet limbs
glistening absorbed in the same idle fun
that hasn't changed in forty summers
of watchful mothers who fret for weeks
then shirk in earnest rituals of sunscreen
unhitch their leads & unmuzzle tongues
let chins wag & run about everything

in particular under the cavalier sun
mothers and now fathers too who
knew and played with you recognize
your husband and son yet won't say
hello their memories too fresh filled
too close to the brim with all the kids
there besides what would they say
when every wildwet child far from
fading imagines no end to this day?

trees like druids encircle the pond
their long dark robes lengthen
as parents warn in vain trying
to separate their own offspring
from the mesmerized swarm:
ten minutes till we have to go
why didn't anyone say

after best of luck godspeed
and a handful of rice oh and
by the way there will be some
seriously deep shit to wade through
and I don't just mean the end of bliss...
would it have helped to unwrap that gift
or is knowledge nothing but fear?

driving home at dusk through the village
you always ask to slow down as we pass
the new-lit windows so you can catch
a glimpse albeit fleeting
of other families being themselves
their masks hung on mudroom hooks
their faces luminous as dinner plates
aglow with uneaten food and conversations
that couldn't possibly be anything like ours

Six Caveats upon Entering
the Kingdom of Superlatives

insofar the doorlight behind you
has closed its aperture

downsodeep the steep ravine
brings a bottomless sleep

oversoyonder hills eyes fold
more cloth than can be quilted

abovesohigh a throne no deity
could possibly survive the fall

moonsobright fields glow like seas
of love between continents of trees

insomuch less is more please
leave your dreams at the door

Sidebar

even then you were getting
the feeling that ours would   white glove
be the generation to clean

up the mess the morning after
gather together nostalgia's   slaughter
half-empty bottles no longer

isolated in ghettos or grottos
but scattered on a global schema   cash for gold
ours would be called upon

to fix the clock of ramification
wearing coveralls & respirators   bongwater
dredge knee deep sludge

with a newfangled nanotech
panacea of pure thought   monkeywrench
in hand stalk self-love across

a desolate binary hi-def plain
or muscle our way past   jambase
atrophy back to rhapsody

every dawn a call to arms
to finally apply old school   wrap
charms the boy stitches his

own skin gashed by the baby
he let play with broken glass   infant-guile
the bundle he once was the one

not only to find the hay-hid
needle but thread and   Seuss-Monet
complete the ellipsis of

Lazarus back from the living
who died to tell the tale upon   et tu Enkidu?
return will he say the dead make

better friends with their
counterpart's capacity for   pseudohip
disbelief & therefore wonder

missing the blue morpho
masquerading as an angel   yo Nabokov
suspended in shadow-

forest where light mist
whispers low & vaulted   ensue
canopies seal what seems

from what is merely real
we'll renegotiate the lease   parvenu
on heaven let's make a deal

Words Like Children

love what hovers
    what's come between
        & gone a midday squall

bookended by blue skies
    intravenous shadows
        on a paper wall

fleeting inconsequential
    but don't tell the shōji
        or the sun who until

this moment wasn't sure
    it existed don't tell
        the boy & girl whose every

opus rises & falls on hollow
    bones of insurrection
        birdsong at the start &

end of a day so infinite
    twilight misremembers
        morning's grasp as they trip

hand in seamless hand down
    a garden lane toward...
        don't tell the maker whose

lips grazed your cheek
    whose unseen alchemy
        tends the embers of your

tongue in a lair at once
    familiar & dire & bigger
        even than the hole god

left whatever you do don't
    pull over stop admire the view
        do not dare not to dare to do

Scharp, slyttyng & frotyng

—sic evitabile fulmen

thick slices of brown bread late
November rain aspiring to snow
shot twice in the chest at close range

with blanks he lives to page through
another day's typos exactly who
are his friends why do angels' teeth

never leave marks or infer wings
though we sense small birds
fluttering in our epic hearts

blind necromancer foretell how their
bodies move & space replaces itself
entranced by sudden absence

their dance tracing constellations
night after fatidic night in transit
across untranslatable lives

why was grace a failed factory
abandoned brunt of irony's children
jaded before their tweens what did

the florid aquaholic mean when
he slurred *all that glitters is gone*
how fortunate the brute segue

from good to bad & back again
from harsh piercing & grating
to honeyed liltings amid lemon

laws of pocket-change laughter
jingling pleats smooth the village lap
dancer neckdeep in hearsay we turn

a key to release this world's energy
some days quatrain others couplet
some rhyme with cheeky bastard

others monologue in extended
hexameter & gambol off leaving
the bed unmade the page bereft

he'd like to give his kids some
useful modicum of what if not
health self-reliance integrity wisdom

what? a good nose to tell shit from art
here's what he knows of art:
line drawing on the back of a napkin

impart passion to paddywack
dad's knackered indifference
the onionman's daily dump runs

buried legion of deferred minions
the most he musters: pull over
litter & pay the posted fine no

trademark superhero stuff
no cape or head-snug hoodie
tolerance nay forbearance if

not invaluable the more likely
lesson and maybe most of all
resilience hypocrisy the norm

the superciliousness
just before the storm

This Morning by the River

—for Sarah

a couple standing in the
middle of a new-turned field
above them an enormous

glider broad as a heron's span
swoops in lowering circles
closer to them

closer to the earth until
it comes to rest at their feet
it's then I notice

the small child standing
alongside them and the
scene all coheres

not that they need
a reason for being there
alone together

the father he bears
a certain resemblance
the woman never turns

to face me though I know
she is you
the way she crouches

to speak with the child
and the affirmation?
(without making too much

ecstasy of a spring morning)
gives its rare unsolicited
reply as the man

bends to lift those giant
wings and ready them
for another flight

Blue 44

It might seem like something funny, but, you know, I'm thinking that this blue landscape is more serious than we first believed.—Alexander Melamid

the basics are all here
        eat sleep fuck
                the source of water

but then comes the low
        anthem a shy kid who
                skids into view with his

hat of a question in hand
        quoting the million shades
                of imprecision between map

and the now you never
        draw or visit the vast
                desert between meaning

and insight navigable
        only by night
                water's perfect imperfection

upon which all our names
        are writ libraries museums
                universities and theaters

built in their honor what
        we used to call churches
                the portrait so real everyone

mistakes it for a photo until
        you look at the eyes which
                no one yet has gotten right

Viva la Vida

*Feet, what do I need you for
when I have wings to fly?*—Frida Kahlo

flowers stew too
long in their vases
the dried orchid's
brittle leather stalk
optimistic to a fault
smile and the world
smiles too until it
doesn't

ping pong ball toy
hammer a stray train
or two scattered
as evidence the child
in us still rises ahead
of the rest to color
the coming light

horror of the mudroom
closet floor a jumbled
anarchy of footwear
muckboots & flip flops
toddler crocs & soccer cleats
impossible to tell what's
what or who's whose
nevermind find a mate
more proof we still
have feet even if yours
are dancing shoeless
with the stars

Duende

water boils and oil burns
        silent civilizations of
                trees fall and rise

planes criss-cross a sky
        claiming to be virgin
                each day we pretend

to forget about stars
        then act surprised when
                old friends still sing to us

every day we make it
        into the Guinness book
                & tomorrow rewrite it

all over again only smugger
        let's see who can chug
                the most stout and still

walk the greased pole
        what drives editors
                happily nuts keeps

scribblers in business
        & the rest of us in
                stitches this revision

of precision striving
        drowning & reviving
                driving black sounds

deep down clambering
        up & ever onward
                just beyond our sight

fate & folly entwined
        our sweet dream of
                endless fucking night

Diminuendo

the slender willow stick
takes root without roots
sprouts without a hint
of vegetative promise

grafts itself to another
simply because the two
kissed during a gentle
summer shower

gradually you allow
yourself to wear
the color red again

raise an eyebrow
at passing narratives

even laugh at
a drunken French
actor's indiscretion
juste pour rigoler

the world's non sequiturs
return flushed and breathless
prodigal hecklers who've
walked miles of unmown
fields sleeping children
slung across their backs

re. the rest of your life
thanks but I'll have to
take a rain check
it's nothing personal

we can't all be lovers
alone on a moondeck
shining like a scimitar
adrift on a black sea

gradually the current
repossesses real estate
a little more light leaks
through night's pores

each day you remove
one artifact at a time
small waves sigh and caress
the sand like a tired masseuse

fold & stow the quilt
sort a stack of books
no one else will read
archive memories &
companion emotions

that no longer apply
thank her for being so
fastidious vatic indifferent
to the past while we

played Terrapin Station
in its entirety nostalgia
& amnesia at tug of war

their rope stretched across
an empty abyss that won't
be backfilled by kids' cant

deadlocked until trust
slackens both hands and
synchronizes surrender
replete and reabsorbed

the river glinting below us
wind & sun drying the land's
comely face after last night's
storm shook the spirit free

when least expected a music
intercedes entreating the sky
to change its name to yours

Green Flash

love's all or nothing ultimatum
wanting to die on a regular basis
but not kill yourself
logistics too messy
using a maul to core an apple
an axe to peel it
plus you can still envision
the flip side of the dream
the green flash after sunset
only a few of us see
everyone else turned away
to let night accept day's apology
for what we failed to praise
the loaf rising in the oven
not just ingredients in a bowl
the butter spread golden
on warm slices
the yeasty sex in your mouth
the steam

What hope have these two

of passing in proximity
      let alone meeting
           let alone touching

           tandem trajectories
      randomly ricocheting
from bumper to bumper

building to building
      street by inarticulate
           street let alone catching

           each other's gaze through
      a bus window from coiled
spring to rubbernecked

neighbors racking up high
      scores of lone striving
           knees clutched in fetal

           abeyance of spaces between
      wild excitement & bewilder-
ment of flippers & bells

curled in shining isochrome
      shells let alone colliding
           let alone passion getting

           bounced around anxious
      zinging & zooming
back & forth betting

on a fast-fingered
      kid to keep a cool head
           and make this quarter last

Some Far Country

Their greenness is a kind of grief. —Philip Larkin

what really sucks:
all the clichés are true
the dead want to make
an example of us
we begin to levitate
only upon their cue

you never told me
you could translate fire
you who are as young as ever

dark sacred morning
rain barrel filled to the brim
mirror-black surface
belies another life below

things as they are
without question or reason
no string or Cartesian
theory here is the hand
you're dealt now play it
here is the shape of cloud
now color it in

a giant luna flapping against
the bedroom window last night
his pee-soaked diaper this morning
rest assured you're not missing
a thing even today's anomaly
of blue sky you've been it all before
the doorstep's newborn lung of air
followed by the spider's thread
swept across your face the dog &
cat turning hopeful circles to be
let out sun burning off the luminous
sheet of valley mist from within
I fall asleep with the light on

my tent moves every night
always on the fringe
and even that is too close
the roadway empty save
for trucks hauling sand & stone
back upstream to fill in
washed out roads hourglass
we tip & tip again unseen
rituals of desperation my pen
is a dream meandering through
country I once knew
and will never visit

we travel the same river
in opposite directions
I in the water floating
with the current you
on the horsepath dragging
your barge of family upstream
we pass each other daily
our children wave to me
from the boat & sometimes
offer a hand to pull me on
board for a mile or two
until you notice the added
load and I slip away again
with the flow and swim
to the opposite shore
where bindlestiffs have
set up camp along the banks
soon we will bivouac
beside them and put Paris
out of our minds for good

gossamers you weave
and leave stitched upon
the canvas of our
waking sentience

I write to fill your silence

Amber

Here we are, trapped in the amber of the moment.
—Kurt Vonnegut

right where you wannabe
        lawn mown family in
                rare cohesion famished

around a picnic table
        tucking in to Henry James'
                favorite two words and

a cool pond looming
        like damp gauze
                on your fevered brow

all your restless djinns
        escaping on the high
                arc of a cicada's song

into amniotic air
        too rare to drink
                whelmed in manna

the season finally
        sussed unconscious
                of its own shadow

sprawled across the lush
        sward early & late
                sun & moon coalesce

in the same sky
        kiss hellogoodbye
                on the stoop of toosoon

for even the kids to see
        as if for the first time
                as if at & for the last